AUTISM-FRIENDLY PARENTING

TO RAISE A JOYFUL AUTISTIC CHILD,PRACTICE LOVING AND TRANQUIL PARENTING

BY AURA L. BENNETH

Table of content

Chapter 1

The Reality of Autism

The neurological disorder known as an autism spectrum disorder (ASD) is common. Although some adults with lesser symptoms go untreated, it can be recognized as early as age 2. A kind of autism is four times more likely to emerge in males than in girls. There is a lot of inaccurate information available, and ASD is complicated. Any medical condition may suffer unforeseen, long-lasting impacts from incorrect assumptions. We're going to educate you on the fundamentals of adult autism and dispel some myths. Let's get going!

Autism Explained

ASD refers to a collection of disorders that exhibit difficulties with speech, communication, repetitive behavior, and social interactions. It has a wide range of impact levels, related conditions, and subtypes. Some will require constant support, others do not and can live freely. Although other factors increase the likelihood of someone being born with it, genetics is usually a factor.

Teenagers with ASD may behave differently from children of the same age. ASD symptoms in teenagers include:

1. Clumsiness
2. conversational difficulties
3. recognizing the feelings of others
4. difficulties with emotion regulation
5. Recurring actions
6. Unwanted noises, such as continuously cleaning their throat
7. Having trouble understanding jokes or sarcasm

Males are more likely to have ASD, but it's unclear why. According to several studies, people with ASD have more masculine-looking brain anatomies. Others claim that because the assessment is centered on male traits, more women may receive incorrect diagnoses.

"Vaccines are linked to autism."
In actuality, vaccines do not cause autism. A British surgeon's initial 1997 study is invalid. Numerous research has also disproved this notion.

"Bad parenting is the cause of autism."
Truth: In the great majority of situations, ASD is genetically predisposed. This absurdity was exacerbated by the 1950s "Refrigerator Mother" idea, which claimed that ASD was caused by moms who lacked emotional warmth.

"You are mentally impaired if you have ASD."
ASD can refer to a wide range of outstanding skills as well as difficulties. People who have been diagnosed can have IQs that range from average to high.

Chapter 2

Defining Autism

Developmental impairment known as an autism spectrum disorder (ASD) is brought on by variations in the brain. People with ASD may struggle with confined or repetitive activities or interests, as well as social communication and engagement. Additionally, people with ASD may learn, move, or pay attention in various ways. It is crucial to remember that some individuals without ASD may also experience some of these symptoms. However, these traits can make life very difficult for those with ASD. Regardless of race and nationality, culture, or economic status, ASD affects people everywhere.

Communication and social interaction patterns alter under certain settings.

People with ASD frequently exhibit repetitive and constrained interests or behavioral patterns.

Social contact and social communication
Examples of social interaction and communication traits connected to ASD include

1. eschews or breaks eye contact

2. does not respond to name by the age of nine months
3. does not display joyful, sad, angry, or astonished facial expressions by the age of nine months.
4. not engaging in simple interactive games like pat-a-cake by the age of 12 months
5. By the age of one year, makes few or no gestures (for example, does not wave goodbye)
6. by the age of 15 months, does not share interests with others (for example, shows you an object that they like)
7. by the age of 18 months, does not point to show you something intriguing.
8. at the age of 24 months, does not recognize when others are harmed or unhappy.
9. by the age of 36 months, does not observe or engage in play with other children.
10. at the age of 48 months, does not pretend to be someone else during play, such as a teacher or a superhero.
11. not perform for you in song, dance, or acting by the age of 60 months

Behaviors or Interests that are Restricted or Repetitive

People with ASD can exhibit peculiar habits or hobbies. ASD differs from conditions that are only characterized by issues with social interaction and communication by these behaviors or interests.

Examples of restricted or repetitive ASD-related activities and interests include

1. a youngster playing on the carpet with toy blocks in close-up.
2. sets toys or other items in a line and becomes irate if the order is changed.
3. repeatedly uses the same words or phrases (called echolalia)
4. uses the same playstyle with toys every time.
5. is concentrated on object components (for example, wheels)
6. upset by even little changes
7. possesses obsessions
8. must adhere to specified procedures
9. Has unexpected reactions to sounds, smells, tastes, sights, or feelings. Flaps hands, rocks body, or spins around.

Additional Features

Most people with ASD also exhibit other similar traits. These could consist of

1. delayed linguistic abilities
2. talents for moving slowly
3. delayed abilities in learning or thinking
4. Inattentive, impulsive, or hyperactive behavior
5. a seizure or epilepsy disorder
6. unusual patterns of eating and sleeping
7. digestive disorders (for example, constipation)

8. unusual emotional or mood swings
9. excessive concern, tension, or anxiety
10. Lack of fear or unexpectedly high levels of fear

It is crucial to remember that children with ASD might not exhibit all of the behaviors that were given as examples above.

There are now five separate ASD specifiers, or subtypes, recognized by the DSM-5. As follows:

- ☐ accompanied by another neurodevelopmental, mental, or behavioral disease with catatonia
- ☐ with or without accompanying intellectual impairment
- ☐ with or without accompanying linguistic impairment,
- ☐ with or without other known medical, genetic, or environmental conditions.

One or more specifiers may be identified in a diagnostic of a person.

Before the DSM-5, autistic people can have been given the following diagnoses:

- diagnosis of autism
- Asperger's disorder
- Unspecified pervasive developmental disorder (PDD-NOS)

disorder of disintegration in children

A person who obtained one of these prior diagnoses has not lost their diagnosis and will not require reevaluation, which is crucial to highlight.

The DSM-5 defines ASD as a wide diagnostic that includes disorders like Asperger's syndrome.

Once diagnosed with autism, a person will experience one of the following two conditions:

1. Low perfusion (Reduced blood flow to the brain)

The neurological imbalance or altered neural capabilities in the hypo-perfusion situation are mostly brought on by either induced hypoxia, which is a lack of oxygen that prevents general brain activities or by allowing the buildup of neurotransmitters that affect neuron growth.

2. Impaired immunity (Immune inflammation)

Immune dysregulation (immune inflammation): Children with autism frequently have chronically suppressed immune systems (the brain becomes inflamed). In the digestive system, immune dysregulation is quite obvious. Neuron development is hampered by brain inflammation.

Chapter 3

What brings on autism?

ASD's precise origin is unknown. There is no single cause, according to the most recent study. among the hypothesized ASD risk factors are:

1. having an autistic relative within a close family
2. specific genetic changes
3. hereditary diseases such as fragile X syndrome
4. having elderly parents
5. a little birth weight
6. hormonal imbalances
7. exposure to environmental contaminants and heavy metals
8. viral infection history in the mother
9. exposure of the drugs to the fetus thalidomide or valproic acid (Thalomid)

The National Institute of Neurological Disorders and Stroke (NINDS)Trusted Source claims that a person's propensity for ASD may be influenced by both heredity and environment.

But numerous sources, both new and old trusted Sources, have concluded that immunizations do not cause ASD.

A contentious study from 1998 suggested a connection between autism and the MMR vaccine (measles, mumps, and rubella). But later, in 2010, that paper was retracted after being refuted by more research. Learn more about the risk factors for autism.

What exams are used to identify autism?

A diagnosis of ASD entails:

- multiple screenings
- genetic testing and analyses
- developmental examinations The earlier ASD is discovered in youngsters, the better. Early diagnosis and support may be beneficial for them. The distinction between screening and diagnosis must be made. Children that test positive for ASD may not have the disorder. Additionally, not all autistic children are always detected during testing.

- testing DNA for genetic disorders behavioral assessment
- testing for vision and hearing to rule out any conditions unrelated to an ASD occupational therapy evaluation

Chapter 4

Austim and other afflictions

Numerous physical and mental health issues typically coexist with autism. They consist of the following, but are not limited to:

- GI (gastrointestinal) issues
- Epilepsy
- feeding problems
- disturbed slumber
- Hyperactive/attention-deficit disorder (ADHD)
- Anxiety\Depression
- Disorder of compulsive behavior (OCD)
- Schizophrenia
- Disorder of the mind
- Dwarf Syndrome (DS)
- gastrointestinal (GI) diseases and autism

- **GI (gastrointestinal) issues**

Youngsters with autism are approximately eight times as likely to get GI issues than regular children.
They frequently consist of:

- ☐ persistent constipation
- ☐ Continent pain
- ☐ stomach acid reflux

- ☐ Bowel discomfort
- ☐ Medical guidelines have been created by the Autism Speaks Autism Care Network (ACN) to assist physicians in identifying and treating these problems.

- **Epilepsy and autism**

Up to one-third of individuals with autism have epilepsy (seizure disease). In comparison, just 1% to 2% of the overall population is impacted.

1. Red flags consist of:
   - ☐ mysterious staring spells
   - ☐ uncontrollable motions
   - ☐ Unknown confusion
   - ☐ bad headaches
2. Less specific symptoms could be:
   - ☐ Sleepiness
   - ☐ disturbed slumber
   - ☐ Unexpected changes in skills or feelings

- **feeding and eating problems and autism**

About 7 out of 10 children with autism struggle with feeding and eating issues.

Extremely restrictive eating patterns and allergies to particular flavors and textures are just two examples of these problems. Similar food dislikes and restrictive eating habits are reported by many adults with autism.

These difficulties are frequently brought on by hypersensitivities associated with autism and/or a high craving for similarity.

The problem of persistent overeating resulting in obesity is another. It may result from a lack of the ability to recognize when one is "full" and/or from using food as a calming behavior.

Pica, or eating non-food objects, is a particularly risky behavior frequently linked to autism. It seems to afflict those with autism the most frequently.
Many autism clinics offer specialized eating programs staffed by behavioral therapists and dietitians, such as those in the Autism Speaks ACN. Some speech, behavioral, and occupational therapists can assist outside of such programs.

- **Autism and sleep disturbances**

Four out of five autistic children, or more than half of them, may suffer from chronic sleep issues.

Similar difficulties with falling asleep and remaining asleep all night are common among adults on the spectrum. These sleep problems frequently exacerbate behavioral difficulties, obstruct learning, and lower general quality of life.

- **Attention deficit and hyperactivity disorder and autism (ADHD)**

Compared to 6–7% of the general population, 30–60% of people with autism are thought to have ADHD.

When it comes to school and daily life, ADHD is characterized by a recurring pattern of inattention, memory loss, difficulties organizing one's time, hyperactivity, and/or impulsivity.

The signs of autism and ADHD can coexist. Because of this, it may be challenging to identify ADHD in a person on the autism spectrum.

- **anxiety and autism**

Up to 42% of individuals with autism have anxiety issues. In contrast, they are thought to afflict 15% of adults and 3% of children in the overall population.

Behavior frequently offers the best cues in those experiencing anxiety because those with autism spectrum disorders may struggle to recognize and communicate their feelings. A racing heart, tight muscles, and stomach problems are among symptoms of anxiety. Some people even report feeling immobile.

Autism sufferers are particularly prone to social anxiety, which is characterized by an intense fear of unfamiliar individuals, crowds, and social situations. A lot of autistic persons also struggle to regulate their anxiety after it is triggered.

At different times and through various activities, including some that were previously joyful, anxiety might be brought on.

- **Depression and autism**

An estimated 7% of children and 26% of adults with autism suffer from depression. Comparatively, it affects 7% of adults and 2% of children in the general population.

Autism-related depression rates increase with age and intelligence. Communication difficulties associated with autism can conceal depression. Loss of interest in once-favorite hobbies, a discernible decline in cleanliness, persistent emotions of melancholy, hopelessness, worthlessness, and anger are all warning indicators that something is wrong. Depression can be so severe that it frequently leads to thoughts of suicide or death.

- **Disorder of compulsive behavior (OCD)**

According to research, teens and adults with autism are more likely than the general population to have OCD.

However, it can be challenging to tell the difference between OCD symptoms and the repetitive actions and constrained interests that characterize autism.

- **Schizophrenia and Autism**

Both autism and schizophrenia have difficulties interpreting language and comprehending the emotions and thoughts of others. The psychosis associated with schizophrenia, which frequently incorporates hallucinations, is an obvious distinction. Additionally, schizophrenia first manifests in early adulthood, whereas the fundamental symptoms of autism often appear between 1 and 3 years of age.

- **Bipolar disorder co-occurs with autism**

Mania—a frenetic state known as bipolar disorder—and depressive episodes frequently occur back-to-back in those with the illness.

By examining the onset and duration of the symptoms, it is crucial to distinguish between those of real bipolar disorder and those of autism. For instance, a child with autism may exhibit constant high energy and invasive social behavior throughout childhood. As a result, rather than being a sign of a manic mood fluctuation, her propensity to chat with strangers and make inappropriate comments is probably a feature of her autism.

Autism and Down syndrome (DS-ASD)
According to research, 16–18% of individuals with Down syndrome also have autism spectrum disorder (Richards et al., 2015).

When Down syndrome is present together with autism, additional Down syndrome symptoms, such as social and behavioral impairments, communication problems, and restricted interests, may be seen (intellectual disability, speech and language delays).

Chapter 5

parenting advice for children with autism

Living with an autistic person comes with a lot of responsibilities, which puts families under a lot of stress. Siblings may feel embarrassed or forgotten, parents must deal with behaviors and pursue treatments while also making plans for the future, and the entire family must be active in the community. Everyone involved, including parents, siblings, grandparents, extended family, and friends, will benefit much from understanding and preparing for the challenges ahead.

Making Your Autistic Child Thrive

If you just found out that your child has autism spectrum disorder or may have it, you're undoubtedly wondering and fretting about what happens next. A diagnosis of ASD can be especially terrifying since no parent is ever ready to learn that their child is anything other than happy and healthy. You could be perplexed by conflicting treatment recommendations or unaware of how to best assist your child. You could also be concerned that nothing you do will change because you've been informed that ASD is an incurable, lifelong disorder.

Even though it's true that ASD isn't something a person just "grows out of," there are a lot of strategies that can help kids learn new abilities and get through several developmental obstacles. To fulfill your child's specific needs and enable them to learn, develop, and flourish in life, support is available, including free government services, in-home behavioral treatment, and school-based programs.

It's essential to look after oneself while caring for a child with ASD. Being emotionally resilient enables you to provide the greatest care possible for your child. These basic knowledge can ease the burden of raising a child who has autism.

- ☐ Stop waiting for a diagnosis.

The best thing you can do as a parent of a kid with ASD or associated developmental delays is to begin therapy as soon as possible. As soon as you suspect a problem, get assistance. Don't hold off to see if your youngster will eventually catch up or outgrow the issue. Waiting for a formal diagnosis is unnecessary. The better the possibility of treatment success for children with autism spectrum disorder, the earlier they receive assistance. The best strategy to accelerate a child's growth and lessen autism symptoms over time is through early intervention.

- ☐ Having an autistic child

Study up on autism. The more knowledgeable you are about autism spectrum conditions, the more able you will be to make choices for your child. Ask questions, become knowledgeable about the available treatments, and take part in choosing your treatment.

- ☐ Gain expertise in your child. Find out what causes your child's difficult or disruptive behaviors and what makes them go away. What frightens or stresses out your child? Calming? Uncomfortable? Enjoyable? Understanding how your child is affected will help you solve issues more effectively and prevent or alter challenging situations.

- ☐ Embrace your child's differences. Practice acceptance rather than focusing on how your autistic child differs from other kids and what he or she is "missing." Enjoy your child's unique traits, acknowledge tiny victories, and refrain from comparing your child to others. More than anything else, your child will benefit from feeling welcomed and loved unconditionally.

- ☐ Never give up. The trajectory of autism spectrum conditions cannot be predicted. Don't assume anything about how your child's life will turn out. People with autism have a lifetime to mature and hone their skills, just like everyone else.

You can assist a youngster with autism spectrum disorder (ASD) in overcoming their difficulties in a variety of ways. The first of these parenting hints is:

1.Ensure stability and safety
Your child will benefit greatly from your involvement in treatment and your efforts to learn as much as you can about autism. The following advice will also help you and your kid with ASD live more comfortably at home:

2. Be dependable
Children with ASD struggle to transfer their knowledge from one environment, like the classroom or therapist's office, to another, like their home. For instance, your child might communicate with you at home using sign language, but not at school. The most effective strategy to support learning is to provide stability in your child's environment. Learn what the therapists are doing with your child and use the same methods at home. To help your child apply what he or she has learned from one environment to another, consider having treatment take place in more than one location. It's crucial to maintain consistency in how you speak to your child and handle difficult behaviors.

3. Follow a timetable
Children with ASD typically function best when they follow a routine or schedule that is very structured. This relates once more to the consistency they both require and desire. Establish a routine for your child's meals, therapy sessions, school hours, and bedtime. Try to limit

the number of times this process is interrupted. If a schedule change is unavoidable, get your youngster ready for it in advance.

4. Honor good conduct
With children with ASD, positive reinforcement can go a long way, so try to "catch them doing something good." Be extremely explicit about the conduct you're praising them for when you congratulate them when they behave appropriately or when they master a new ability. Consider additional methods of rewarding them for excellent behavior, such as letting them play with a favorite item or giving them a sticker.

5. Establish a home security zone
Create a personal area in your home where your youngster may unwind, feel comfortable, and feel secure. This calls for structuring and establishing limits in a way that your child can comprehend. Visual clues may prove useful (colored tape marking areas that are off limits, labeling items in the house with pictures). Additionally, you might want to safety-proof your home, especially if your kid is prone to tantrums or other self-harming behaviors.

6. Use nonverbal communication to connect
It can be difficult to connect with a child who has ASD, but you don't have to talk or even touch to bond. Your body language, tone of voice, how you look at your child, and sometimes even how you touch them are all ways that you can connect with them. Even if your child

never speaks, they are talking with you anyway. All you have to do is study the language.

7. Observe nonverbal cues
You can learn to recognize the nonverbal clues that kids with ASD use to communicate if you are alert and watchful. When a person is tired, hungry, or in need of anything, you may tell by the sounds they make, their facial expressions, and the actions they make.

8. Determine the cause of the temper outburst.
When you are misunderstood or disregarded, it's only normal to feel sad, and this is also true for children with ASD. Children with ASD frequently act out when you fail to notice their nonverbal cues, according to research. Their method of expressing their annoyance and demanding your attention is through tantruming.

9. Schedule an enjoyable time
Despite having ASD, a child is still a child. There must be more to life than therapy for both parents and children with ASD. Decide when your child will be most awake and alert for fun. Consider the things that make your child laugh, smile, and come out of her/his shell as you try to come up with methods to have fun together. If these activities don't seem therapeutic or instructional, your youngster is most likely to enjoy them. Both you and your child will gain a lot by taking pleasure in one another's presence and spending time together unhurriedly. All children need to play to learn, and it shouldn't feel like work.

10. consider your child's sensory sensitivity.
Many kids with ASD have extreme sensitivity to touch, sound, light, smell, and taste. Some autistic children exhibit "under-sensitivity" to sensory stimuli. Analyze your child's "bad" or disruptive actions to see what sights, sounds, smells, movements, and tactile sensations they are drawn to, as well as what makes them feel good. What causes stress in your child? Calming? Uncomfortable? Enjoyable? You'll be more adept at solving issues, averting sticky situations, and fostering positive experiences if you know what impacts your child.

11. Develop a specialized autism treatment strategy
It might be difficult to decide which treatment is best for your child when there are so many options available. You can receive various or even contradicting advice from your parents, professors, and doctors, further complicating the situation.

Remember that no single treatment is effective for everyone when creating a treatment plan for your child. Every autistic individual is different, with unique talents and shortcomings.

The course of treatment for your child should be personalized for their particular need. It is up to you to see that their needs are satisfied because you are the one who knows your child the best. You can achieve it by posing the following inquiries to yourself:

12. Remember that your participation is essential to the success of any treatment strategy you choose.
By collaborating with the treatment team and completing the therapy at home, you can ensure that your kid gets the most out of their treatment. (This is why it's crucial to prioritize your health!)

Following a step by step procedure

- Build on your child's interests in a good therapy strategy.
- Provide a foreseeable schedule.
- Teach tasks in small, manageable increments.
- Engage your child's interest directly in activities that are quite structured.
- Give behavior reinforcement regularly.
- Participate the parents.
- selecting autism therapies
- Behavioral therapy, speech-language therapy, physical therapy, occupational therapy, and nutritional therapy are just a few of the various treatments and methods used to treat ASD.

Note: It's doubtful that you'll be able to treat all of your child's issues at once, even while you're not required to restrict your child to just one treatment at a time. Instead, begin by concentrating on your child's urgent needs and most severe symptoms.

13. Obtain aid and assistance
A child with ASD can require a lot of time and effort to care for. There may be times when you feel stressed,

discouraged, or overburdened. Raising a child with special needs is even harder than parenting a typical youngster. You must look after yourself if you want to be the best parent you can be.

Don't attempt to handle everything by yourself. You're not required to! Families of children with ASD have a variety of resources at their disposal for guidance, assistance, advocacy, and support:

- ☐ ASD support groups - Attending an ASD support group is a terrific opportunity to connect with other families going through similar struggles. Parents can rely on one another for emotional support, information sharing, and advice. The isolation many parents face after learning their child has a diagnosis can often be much diminished by simply being around others who are in the same situation and listening to their stories.

14.Every parent requires a break from time to time. This is especially true for parents dealing with the additional stress caused by ASD. Respite care allows you to take a break for a few hours, days, or even weeks by temporarily replacing you with another caregiver. This is when your child is cared for by another person for a while, either inside your home, outside, or both so that you can take a quick break. You'll require it, particularly if your child has severe demands as a result of ASD. This can provide you the chance to engage in activities that improve your health and that you love, enabling you to return home ready to assist. These techniques can be used to choose or create your respite support team: Ask your friends, relatives, and other parents you know for any possible support links.

15. Seek advice or recommendations from your child's physicians, therapists, and educators. For example, a teacher's assistant you truly like might adore watching children in their spare time.

16. You can also advertise for child care help in local religious organizations, periodicals, online, and at schools and institutions close to you. Make sure you thoroughly review all references.

17. Be a part of a parent support group for children with autism. Learn from what has worked for others. A local autism support center can help you identify self-help groups; alternatively, you can search online.

18. Counseling for individuals, couples, or families
You might wish to consult your therapist if stress, anxiety, or depression are starting to affect you. Therapy is a secure setting where you can openly discuss all of your feelings, good, terrible, and ugly. Marriage and family counseling can also assist you in resolving issues that the difficulties of raising an autistic kid are producing in your marriage or with other family members.

19. Services in special education (age three and older)
Assistance is provided to children over three through school-based initiatives. Special education programs are adapted to your child's unique requirements, just as early intervention. Children with ASD are frequently placed in small groups with other children who are developmentally delayed so that they can receive more individualized care and specialized training. But they might also spend at least some of the school day in a conventional classroom, depending on their skills. The idea is to put children in the "least restrictive environment" they can be in while still learning.

20. Recognize your kid's rights
You have the following legal rights as the parent of a kid with ASD:

- Participate in the entire IEP process for your child.
- disagree with the recommendations of the educational system
- Get your youngster evaluated by a third party.

You can ask anyone you wish to be a part of the IEP team, from a family to your child's doctor.
If you think your child's needs are not being fulfilled, you can request an IEP meeting at any time.
If you can't reach a compromise with the 20, you can get free or inexpensive legal representation.
Reduce your stress.

21. ASD parents frequently experience higher levels of stress than parents of children with other disorders.

Caretakers may experience relationship breakdowns and even psychological problems if the problem is not addressed. Your health might also be impacted by stress. Keep your affairs to keep from becoming overburdened. This entails setting aside time each day for oneself. Among the crucial and even enjoyable ways to do it are:

- Determine the true origins of your stress. If you're feeling overwhelmed, divide your main problems into smaller, more manageable portions. You'll have a strategy and feel better.
- Other options include meditation. Be mindful of your inner dialogue as much as your ideas. You'll be able to eliminate pointless concerns.
- Exercise. You are not required to visit the gym. Swim, exercise in the garden, dance in the kitchen, or simply go for a walk. These are quick and efficient ways to work out.
- Take an exercise class if you want some adult company. It's a fantastic way to make new friends and get your energy back.
- Go to sleep. There is no substitute for a restful night's sleep when it comes to rejuvenating your body and mind. Use meditation or relaxation techniques to aid in your relaxation if necessary. That could aid in getting your body ready for sleep.
- Be inventive with your cuisine. You probably put a lot of effort into making sure your child eats well-balanced meals. How are you doing?

Consider experimenting with new fruits, vegetables, and cuisines to spice up your unique food. To keep things fresh, look up new recipes. and adhere to a daily eating routine. You can keep your system on track and your energy levels up.

22. Get your life in balance.
This is the secret to overcoming obstacles in life while maintaining a high standard of living. You and your family will all gain. Schedule some time each week for mingling and having fun. To bring balance to your busy days, try these suggestions:

- Locate your pals. You do indeed have a child with special needs. But you are also a person. Being aware of your individuality helps you be a better parent. Spend some time laughing and reuniting with your buddies. You'll be happy that you did.
- rekindle previous interests. Find your knitting needles, clean the piano, or take the golf clubs out of the bag. Try out some new hobbies that interest you.
- Count to five each day. Spending a few additional minutes in the morning can help you focus and set the tone for the rest of the day. Consider taking a long, warm shower, gathering your thoughts, or writing down some ideas in a journal. Do it quickly.

Chapter 6

Things you shouldn't do when raising a child with autism

When raising a child with autism, there are six things you should not do.
Avoid these parenting approaches.
Autism-related parenting may be both difficult and rewarding.
Children with autism don't interact, play, or behave like their neurotypical peers, and some parents or guardians may find this confusing, annoying, or downright disturbing.
However, children with autism have talents and abilities that can only be seen when a parent is attentive and willing to interact with their child in a way that suits their needs. This means that it's not always advisable to just do what comes naturally to you as a parent or guardian when you have a child with autism.

In other words, you might need to deliberately steer clear of certain parenting practices since they might swiftly sour your bond with a child who is autistic.

1. Parenting by helicopter
Parents who hover over their kids constantly monitor and respond to their every move. When a difficulty is approaching, they step in to assist; they step in to clear

every road, and they insist on special treatment for their offspring.

Any child would benefit from less-than-ideal parenting, as it makes it more challenging for them to develop independence and self-determination.

Because they fear their autistic child will encounter issues they can't handle—which, of course, is entirely possible—parents or guardians of children with autism are more likely to practice helicopter parenting.

However, if helicopter parenting slows down the development of neurotypical children, just think about what it will do to autistic children.

Children with autism must be taught directly and by doing because they are unable to learn by observation or modeling.

When you help them out with their work, you're depriving them of the chance to learn from their mistakes, experience the difficulty of attempting, enjoy the rush of accomplishment, or grasp what is required.

2. Rivalry in parenting
Every parent or guardian who has participated in a Mommy and Me group is well aware of the concept of

competitive parenting. Who trained their infant first? said the initial phrase? Is learning to dance or sing, playing pewee soccer, taking the most lessons, or studying foreign languages?

It might be challenging not to feel as though the child in your care is being left behind when you have a child with autism. However, if you adopt a competitive parenting style, you will undoubtedly come to believe that the child in your care is underachieving and that you, as the parent, are most likely to blame.

As you might expect, the result is a sense that neither you nor the child you are parenting is deserving of success. These emotions do affect a child with autism, even if they may not be immediately apparent.

3. Hands-Off (Free-Range) Parenting

Some parents and guardians feel that their children should be free to pursue their interests without interference from them. That works effectively for certain neurotypical kids who are driven, self-directed, and eager to socialize. However, a youngster with autism shouldn't make this decision.

Even though every child deserves and needs "down" time, children with autism require regular, attentive parental involvement.

That's because most of the time, kids with autism need your assistance to actively learn to pretend, interact with others, have conversations, ask questions, and learn about the outside world.

Without someone to assist them to develop these vital abilities, children with autism may grow more reclusive and self-absorbed, becoming less capable or motivated to interact with others in the outside world. Additionally, they won't have as many chances to develop their advantages and maximize their potential.

4. Tiger (Perfectionist) Parenting

Yes, some kids do well with parents who adamantly demand straight As, top athletic achievement, flawless language, and immaculate table manners. It's doubtful that the kids have autism.

While autistic children may have many strengths, the truth is that they may struggle greatly with many neurotypical childhood expectations. They might not be able to achieve good marks or flawless grammar due to their poor verbal skills. Sports may be particularly challenging for them since they may have trouble with physical coordination.

High expectations are necessary, even for a child with impairments, but if you set them too high, you and the child in your care may experience harmful levels of stress.

5. Allowable Parenting

You may believe as the parent of an autistic child that there should be no expectations for your child outside of school or therapy. After all, autistic children struggle to function in the classroom and need a break.

Even asking the child in your care to do chores, practice self-control, or learn to calm down may seem ridiculous to you. This type of "do whatever you want" parenting has the unintended effect of teaching children habits and behaviors that may lead to major issues in the future.

While having autism may make some things more challenging, kids with autism almost always have a lot they can accomplish when given the chance and encouragement. Setting the bar too low or providing a child with autism with insufficient discipline makes it harder for them to grasp or meet high standards.

Recognizing a youngster's difficulties is one thing; presuming a child is incompetent is quite another and destructive.

6. Activist parenting
A child with autism has received five hours of behavioral therapy, an hour of speech and physical therapy, two hours of parent-led play therapy, and four hours of school since they got out of bed this morning.

You rush online to find yet another therapeutic class, program, activity, or resource to add to the calendar as soon as the kid passes out from exhaustion. With so much going on, the autistic child in your care is unable to put what they have learned into practice, interact with and get to know another child, or simply play like a child.

Consider the notion that a few hours a day of calm, unfocused parent or guardian-and-child time might be all that a youngster needs to grow and thrive rather than feverishly seeking out and participating in therapies and activities.

Message From Verywell

Parents and guardians of children with disabilities are under greater pressure than most because no one is perfect. It might be frightening for some parents or guardians to continually deal with serious behavioral problems like autistic meltdowns.

As a result, you might be less prepared financially or emotionally than the usual parent or guardian and may be more overburdened, exhausted, frustrated, or anxious.

It's perfectly acceptable to ask for help when you're feeling overburdened, whether it comes from other family members, neighbors, or neighborhood organizations that support families with impaired members. Keep in mind that by taking care of yourself, you will be able to support the child in your care the best you can.

Chapter 7

relatives with autism

Siblings of autistic children experience social and emotional difficulties
One of the two female children is sobbing while the other is looking away as they play with blocks.
Solution for siblings: Early behavioral therapy may be helpful for siblings of autistic children.

Siblings at risk:
The researchers looked at 69 studies that included a total of 21,263 controls and 6,679 kids with an autistic sibling. One of the siblings in some of these control pairs has a different developmental disorder or a different kind of handicap.

Siblings of autistic children are more likely to be withdrawn and have poor social skills than siblings of children without the disorder. By a variety of metrics, they also do worse socially and emotionally than siblings of kids with intellectual disabilities or other types of developmental delay.

They are not more likely than controls to exhibit difficulties with external behavior, such as hostility. Additionally, their coping mechanisms are not particularly unique.

According to Molly Losh, associate professor of communication sciences and disorders at Northwestern University in Evanston, Illinois, the findings suggest that siblings of autistic children are at risk for secondary conditions or traits associated with autism but not for the core characteristics of autism, which the researchers did not examine. Losh didn't take part in the investigation. They "indicate comorbid disorders and characteristics that may accumulate in families, and for which siblings may be at risk," she claims.

According to Paige Siper, an assistant professor of psychiatry at the Icahn School of Medicine at Mount Sinai in New York, "Siblings should be assessed for internalizing and other psychiatric disorders, which can be targeted effectively through evidence-based therapies."

thriving while raising a child with autism
Lara Jones, a mother of a six-year-old autistic child
1. Address the environment, not the individual
In the past, parents have attempted to assist their kids by minimizing their autistic behavior and teaching their autistic children to imitate youngsters who aren't autistic.

It may be due to anxiety if a youngster with autism engages in self-stimulating activities ('stimming' - spinning, flailing hands).

"If your goal is to have a happy child, it's preferable to concentrate on ending whatever is making them anxious,"

"If you take away their coping method, stimming, you take that away. By getting your youngster out of a difficult environment, try to decrease the anxiety and work up from there.

2. Recognize the various sensory systems.

The social challenges that might come with autism are well documented, but the sensory challenges that autistic people experience may be less well acknowledged.

When compared to non-autistic persons, this can involve processing sound, sight, touch, smell, and taste differently and receiving too much or too little feedback from these senses.

"This is why taking an autistic child to the store or a music class may be torture for them,"

Consider what it must be like for a child who is unable to block off background noise, witnesses everyone else managing while they are unable to, and is unable to communicate their pain and suffering.

Adapt the current world to your child's requirements because it wasn't created with them in mind.

To do this, don't expect them to join you at loud gatherings if they don't enjoy them; provide them with noise-canceling earbuds if you're going to the grocery store, and take into account why your child cries when brushing their teeth.

She advises parents to communicate whatever modifications they come up with to help their autistic child adjust to their sensory differences with their school.

3. **Address your problems.**

Lara acknowledges that it took her years to accept her son's diagnosis and notes that most parents must fight for an evaluation before fighting cash-strapped local authorities to obtain the proper support at school.

She claims that as a result, the majority of them experience stress and are unable to offer enough help to others.

"Parents who are so distressed that they only discuss their personal experiences—rather than those of their children—are encountered when I attend parents' groups designed to help us learn more about our children.

"

To the point where the agony subsides and you can see your child's needs more clearly, seek support.

She claims that going to a therapist regularly has helped her handle these problems.

4. Plan your life.

Uncertainty is one of the largest challenges for worried autistic children, and while it can't be eliminated in everyday life, it may be reduced at home.

Lara argues that "structure and preparation are your friends."

She advises using visual schedules or writing down a daily schedule if your child is older or less visually inclined. Establish routines by performing the same tasks in the morning in the same order, and repeat the same activities during the summer.
To prepare your child for a new destination, look up pictures online or request that they be emailed to you.

5. Pick your school battles wisely.
According to Lara, little government money makes it difficult for schools to support autistic students' belongings, therefore parents should ensure that what needs to happen is truly happening.
She cautions, "You also need to pick your battles. Focus on what will have the most impact on your child because the school probably won't be able to do all you want them to do or that they should be doing.

6. Talk to adults with autism
Lara emphasizes that individuals with autism are the ones who truly understand the condition.
When doing research for her book, she spoke with a lot of individuals who are autistic, and she claims that it has changed the way she views differences completely.
Now, whenever I'm unsure of how to handle a situation with my son, I message a friend who has autism and always gets wise counsel.

Adapting to and gaining independence in a setting with autistic people

1. Present the Visual Schedule

Your youngster will move from activity to activity more smoothly if you use a visual schedule. With your child, go over each item on the timetable, and then tell him or her to double-check it before each transition. He or she will eventually be able to finish this work more independently, experience making decisions, and engage in the activities they find interesting. Download the ATN/AIR-P Visual Supports and Autism Spectrum Disorder Tool Kit to learn more about using visual supports.

2. Practice self-care techniques

You should start including self-care activities in your child's routine at this age. Activities of daily living (ADLs) such as combing one's hair, brushing one's teeth, and other ADLs are crucial life skills that should be taught to children as early as feasible. To help your youngster get acclimated to having them as part of the daily routine, include these activities in his or her calendar.

3. Encourage Your Child to Request a Break

Ensure that your child has the means to ask for a break by including a "Break" button on any communication devices they may be using, an image in their PECS book, etc. Determine a calm location where your youngster can go if they're feeling stressed. Instead, think about providing headphones or other instruments to assist control sensory input. Understanding how to request a break can help your child regain control over both themselves and their environment, even though it may seem like a small thing.

4. Perform household duties

Giving kids things to do can help them learn responsibility, include them in family activities, and teach them valuable life skills that they can apply as they get older. You might think about doing a task analysis if you believe your youngster may have problems comprehending how to finish an entire task. This technique entails breaking down challenging activities into manageable chunks. Make sure to act as a role model for your youngster or offer guidance if necessary. Consider using My Job Chart as well, which is a fantastic tool for teaching adults and children how to finish things on time.

5. Hone Your Money Skills

The ability to manage money is a crucial one that can help your child become independent when they are out and about in the neighborhood. Whatever talents your child now possesses, there are ways for him or her to start learning about money. Consider including financial literacy in your child's IEP at school, and when you are accompanying your child at a store or supermarket, let him or her give the money to the cashier. You can instruct each step of this method one at a time. Then, your youngster can start applying these abilities in a variety of community contexts.

6. Instruct in Community Safety

Many families have serious safety concerns, especially as kids grow increasingly independent. Teach and practice travel safety lessons, such as how to read signs and other crucial safety indicators and how to use public transit. Numerous helpful hints are included in the GET Going pocket handbook to assist people with autism in using public transit. Consider letting your child carry an ID card that has his or her name, a succinct description of their disease, and a contact number. Examples of ID cards and other excellent safety materials are available.

7. Develop leisure abilities

Your child will benefit from being able to engage in independent leisure and recreation throughout his or her life. It can be helpful to adapt specific interests in one or two topics that many persons with autism have into age-appropriate recreational activities. Team sports, swim lessons, martial arts, music groups, and other activities are among those included in the Autism Speaks Resource Guide for parents to get their children engaged within their local communities. See the Autism Speaks Leading the Way: Autism-Friendly Youth Organizations page for additional details about joining youth and community organizations.

8. Encourage self-care among adolescents

A teenager with autism may experience many changes as they approach puberty and enter adolescence, therefore now is a crucial time to teach them various hygiene and self-care skills. As they approach adulthood, your kids will be a lot more independent if you help them develop the habit of taking care of themselves. To help your kid accomplish his or her daily personal hygiene routine, visual aids can be quite helpful. To assist your child in keeping track of what has to be done, consider creating an activity checklist and posting it in the bathroom. This can involve activities like taking a shower, washing your face, applying deodorant, and combing your hair. You can put together a hygiene "kit" to store all the supplies your child needs in one location to stay organized.

9. Develop your technical skills

Your child's IEP has to incorporate some vocational training beginning at age 14. Make a list of the person's abilities, interests, and talents and use it to inform the kinds of career-related activities that are included as objectives. Starting your future planning now will be beneficial. Take into account all the ways you have up to this point encouraged your child's independence: communication skills, self-care, interests and activities, and future objectives. To develop an individual transition plan for your kid, you can assess their existing skills and abilities using the Community-based Skills Assessment (CSA).

10. Improve Communications

If your child has difficulty speaking, improving communication skills and giving them the means to express preferences, desires, and feelings will be a crucial step in fostering independence. Think about introducing visual aids and alternative/augmentative communication (AAC). Picture Exchange Communication Systems (PECS), speech output devices (such DynaVox, iPad, etc.), and sign language are common forms of AAC.

www.ingramcontent.com/pod-product-compliance
Lightning Source LLC
LaVergne TN
LVHW020524160826
845677LV00015B/3877

* 9 7 9 8 8 4 4 2 2 5 9 8 7 *